S0-BYC-643

Our WILD™ WORLD
SERIES

Seals

NorthWord Press
Chanhassen, Minnesota

To my wife, Aubrey, who loves to swim with the seals
                                                    —W. L.

Illustrations by John F. McGee
Designed by Russell S. Kuepper
Edited by Aimee Jackson

NorthWord Press
18705 Lake Drive East
Chanhassen, MN 55317
1-800-328-3895
www.northwordpress.com

Library of Congress Cataloging-in-Publication Data

Lynch, Wayne.
    Seals / text and photography by Wayne Lynch ; illustrations by John F. McGee.
       p. cm. -- (Our wild world series)
    Summary: Introduces the natural history and life cycle of pinnipeds, commonly known
as seals.
    ISBN 1-55971-827-7 (hardcover) -- ISBN 1-55971-826-9 (softcover)
      1. Pinnipedia--Juvenile literature. [1. Pinnipeds. 2. Seals (Animals)] I. McGee, John F.,
ill. II. Title. III. Series

    QL737.P6 L96 2002
    599.79--dc21   2002019004

Printed in Singapore

10 9 8 7 6 5 4 3 2 1

Seals

Text and photography by Wayne Lynch
Illustrations by John F. McGee

NorthWord Press
Chanhassen, Minnesota

OCEANS COVER almost three-quarters of the surface of the Earth. Because the oceans are so large and filled with food, it is no surprise that many mammals live there. These mammals, called marine mammals, include giant whales, fast-swimming dolphins and porpoises, and plant-munching manatees, which some people call sea cows. There are other marine mammals too, such as fuzzy-faced sea otters, great white polar bears, and pinnipeds (PIN-a-peds). The name pinniped means fin-footed. The pinnipeds are a large group of marine mammals that are commonly known as seals. Everyone can identify a seal, but most don't know that there are 33 species (SPEE-sees), or kinds, of seals. That's a large number of seals to remember. Luckily, all of the seals belong to just three different groups. It is easy to figure out which group a seal belongs to simply by looking at the animal's ears and watching how it swims and moves on land.

There are only about 1300 Hawaiian monk seals, making it one of the rarest seals on Earth.

This crabeater seal in Antarctica is a lucky one. The scars on its side are from an old leopard seal attack.

This southern elephant seal is molting its old skin.
It throws damp sand over its body to help it cool off.

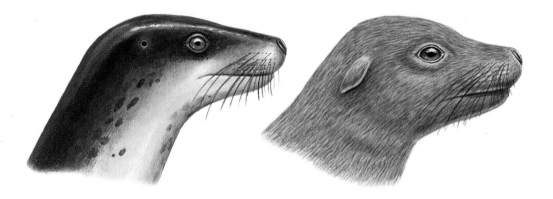

The seals in one group have no external ears, just a small hole on each side of their head through which they hear. Because they appear to have no ears, they are often called the earless seals. This group includes the harp seal, the ringed seal, and the bearded seal. All of the earless seals swim by sweeping their large rear flippers, which are shaped like a fan, from side to side to propel themselves through the water. On land these seals either drag themselves forward by using the strong claws on their small front flippers, or they hump along the ground like a giant caterpillar. Usually the earless seals do not move very fast, nor very far from the water.

This southern elephant seal pup is snoozing on a beach in southern Argentina. The pup will stay on shore for 50 days after its mother abandons it.

A large male California sea lion tries to herd a female into his territory along the beach. The female barks in protest.

The second group of seals is made up of sea lions and fur seals, including Hooker's sea lion, the California sea lion, and the northern fur seal. Sea lions are the seals that circus people train to balance a ball on the end of their nose. All sea lions and fur seals have small curled ear flaps, and they are commonly called the eared seals. Eared seals swim differently than the earless seals. Instead of swimming with their rear flippers, they use their broad front flippers, which are shaped like the blade of a canoe paddle, and they use their rear flippers to steer. On land the eared seals use their rear flippers to walk and run around, and they can do this better than all the other seals. When an Antarctic fur seal is frightened or angry, it can run almost as fast as a human.

The third group of seals includes only one seal, the walrus. This is the easiest seal to recognize because it is the only one that has two long white teeth called tusks. A large pair of tusks on an adult male walrus can be as long as a child's baseball bat, about 26 inches (65 centimeters) long. In the water, the walrus uses both its front and rear flippers to swim. On land, it walks by using its rear flippers in the same way as a fur seal or sea lion, but much slower.

Seals
FUNFACT:

Seals, like many other animals, need several years to grow up before they can mate and raise a family. Most female seals are mature at age four, whereas most male seals don't mate until they are five to seven years of age.

Seals live in all the oceans of the world. Some, such as fur seals and the sea lions of the Galapagos Islands, live in the hot tropics and swim with sea turtles and marine iguanas. Other seals and sea lions live along the Atlantic and the Pacific coasts of the United States and Canada, where it is warm in the summer and cold in the winter. But the greatest number of seals live in the Arctic and the Antarctic, the coldest places on Earth, where winter temperatures often dip below -40 degrees Fahrenheit (-40 degrees Celsius). In the Arctic and the Antarctic, the surface of the ocean may be frozen all year round. Even when the ice melts, the water is still very cold and below the freezing point of 29 degrees Fahrenheit (-1.6 degrees Celsius). Water drains heat from an animal's body much faster than air does, and staying warm in the water is one of the biggest problems that a seal faces. How do most seals stay warm? The answer is blubber. Blubber is a thick layer of fat that forms a blanket under the seal's skin everywhere on its body. On a large blubbery walrus or elephant seal, the fat under its skin may be 4 inches (10 centimeters) thick. That is thicker than a triple cheeseburger!

The Antarctic fur seal has brownish-gray fur as do many eared seals, but some, such as the Australian sea lion, have more silvery-gray fur, and the fur of the female South American sea lion is pale gold in color.

When a walrus gets overheated, it must climb over its buddies to reach the water. As it does, the grumpy sunbathers usually jab him with tusks to hurry him along.

All seals have some fur, but unlike the fur on most other animals, the fur on a seal's body does not help it stay warm in the water. The fur on most seals is too thin to keep them warm, and their skin gets soaked as soon as they dive into the water. However, the fur seals are different. They have one of the thickest fur coats of any mammal. It is so thick that water never soaks through to the animal's skin, and the seal stays warm even in very cold water.

Seals leave the water to rest and to have their young. When they do, they may overheat because of the thick fat or dense fur covering their body. How do seals stay cool? Some pant like a dog to cool themselves, while other seals wave their flippers around like a fan. When a walrus overheats, its skin turns red like a cooked lobster, and it must dive back into the cold water to cool off.

All seals are carnivores (KAR-nuh-vorz) and eat other animals when they are hungry. The three most common foods they eat are fish, squid, and a shrimp-like animal called krill. Scientists can sometimes find out what a seal has been eating by checking the color of its scat, or droppings. When a seal eats fish, its droppings are often grayish white. When it eats krill, its droppings are pink, and when it eats squid, its droppings are yellow.

Seals
FUNFACT:

The smallest seal in the world, the female Galapagos fur seal, weighs just 60 pounds (27 kilograms).
The largest seal, the male southern elephant seal, weighs as much as 11,000 pounds (4990 kilograms).

One seal, the leopard seal of Antarctica, feeds on krill and fish in the winter, but then switches to penguins in the summer. The swift, powerful leopard seal hunts penguins in several different ways. One way is to stalk, or follow, the birds from under thin ice. With this method, an underwater seal follows a bird walking across newly formed ice, breaks through the ice—which can be 3 inches (7.5 centimeters) thick—and grabs the unsuspecting bird. If a penguin spots a leopard seal before it attacks, the bird will freeze with fear until it feels safe enough to continue, sometimes even for over an hour.

A leopard seal can also leap onto ice floes and snatch any careless penguin that is standing near the edge. If a penguin is not close enough to catch, the seal may try to drive the birds off the safety of the ice then pursue them in an underwater chase.

A female seal, such as this ringed seal, is called a "cow," a male is a "bull," a newborn is a "pup," and the area where the seals gather to mate is called a "rookery."

Another hunting method for a leopard seal is to hide between pieces of floating ice near shore. When the penguins return from a fishing trip and head to land, they may swim into the seal's deadly jaws. The most common technique is for a leopard seal to patrol an ice edge where the penguins must leap up out of the water onto the ice in order to reach shore. When the tide is out, the ice edge may be 5 feet (1.5 meters) high and the birds may have to make many leaps before they succeed. Tired penguins are easy targets.

The bearded seal, like all seals, is shaped like a torpedo.
This helps it to move through the water more easily.

Sea lions like to play underwater, circling and
chasing each other as these Australian sea lions are doing.

All seals are expert divers, and all of them can hold their breath for at least 20 minutes or more. Most humans cannot hold their breath for even one minute. What happens inside humans' bodies when they stop breathing? Actually, nothing much changes at all. Their temperature stays the same, their heart keeps beating, and their blood continues to move around inside their bodies as usual. But one important thing does change as humans hold their breath. The oxygen in their blood slowly burns away, and if the oxygen level gets too low, they faint.

When human scuba divers go underwater they carry extra oxygen with them inside tanks strapped to their backs. A seal also carries extra oxygen, but in a different way than a scuba diver. A seal has twice as much blood in its body as a human does, so it can carry more oxygen. A seal also stores extra oxygen in its muscles. Seal meat is black in color for this reason. With so much extra oxygen, a seal can dive for many minutes without breathing.

Two other things happen inside a seal's body that do not happen inside a human when it holds its breath. When a seal dives, its heart slows down and blood flows only to the animal's heart and brain. Very little blood circulates to the rest of its body. In this way, the seal saves the oxygen for the two most important parts of its body, the main engine (the heart) and the central computer (the brain). This allows it to stay underwater even longer.

Most seals can hunt day or night. Even during the day, some seals dive so deeply that no sunlight reaches them, and the water is as black as a moonless night. In the darkness of the deep ocean, a seal depends upon its special eyes and whiskers to find its prey (PRAY), the animals it hunts for food. The eyes of a seal are very large to collect as much light as possible. Seals also have a shiny layer on the back of their eyes that magnifies light. Many land mammals such as cats, dogs, and deer have a similar reflective layer in their eyes, called the tapetum lucidum (ta-PEE-tum LOO-si-dum), which shines brightly at night when they stare at the headlights of a car.

Seals
FUNFACT:

All seals dive, but the best divers are the two biggest seals, the northern and southern elephant seals. One northern elephant seal was recorded diving underwater for two hours, and it reached a depth of 5500 feet (1676 meters).

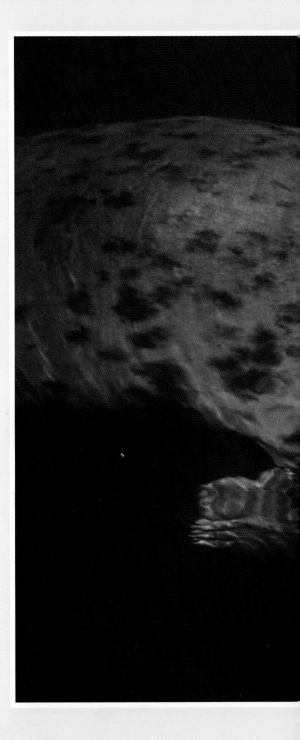

Most seals, including this gray seal, have cone-shaped teeth to help them hold slippery, wiggling prey.

The whiskers on a seal also help it to locate prey in the darkness. A walrus, the most whiskery of the seals, has over 600 thick, stiff whiskers on its floppy upper lip. It uses its whiskers like fingers to feel for sea cucumbers, worms, clams, and crabs hidden in the mud on the ocean bottom. Other seals use their whiskers to detect vibrations in the water when a fish or squid swims nearby. The Antarctic fur seal has only 40 to 60 sensitive whiskers, but some of them may be 18 inches (46 centimeters) long, which is as long as a child's arm.

A walrus never uses its tusks to dig for food.
Instead it uses them to defend itself, chop holes
in the ice, and to haul itself out of the water.

Newborn northern fur seals have black fur when they are born.
Neighboring pups often cluster together when their mothers leave to go fishing.

For most of the year, seals are scattered over the oceans, traveling alone or in small groups. The spring breeding season is the one time of the year when many of them come together in crowds to find a partner. Twenty of the 33 species of seals breed on land (land-breeding seals), while the rest breed on the ice (ice-breeding seals). The seals that breed on land, such as fur seals and sea lions, form the largest groups, or colonies. Millions of Antarctic fur seals may crowd together on the beaches of a single island. A remote island is a good place for a seal colony to gather because there are usually no bears, wolves, humans, or other predators (PRED-uh-tors), animals that hunt other animals for food, to disturb them.

Seals
FUNFACT:

The most threatened seals in the world are the two monk seals: the Hawaiian monk seal and the Mediterranean monk seal, both of which number less than 2000 individuals.

Young southern elephant seals begin to fight when they are less than a year old.
This is serious business and only one in ten adult males will ever grow up to be a father.

Wherever large numbers of land-breeding seals get together, the males usually fight with each other to win female partners. Males, or bulls, chase, wrestle, and slash and tear each other with their sharp teeth. The skin on a bull's neck and shoulders is thick and tough to protect it during such battles.

For the same reason, the neck of a bull walrus is covered with large bumps, a kind of warty armor, to shield itself from the jabs of another walrus's tusks. Even so, many male seals are injured during the battles of the breeding season, and some of them even die.

A male Hooker's sea lion smells the breath of a female. Her breath may identify her and tell him if she is ready to mate.

A male seal will fight to the death for one reason. If he does not, he may never win a mating partner, and so never be the father of a pup, or baby seal. The strongest fighters win the most female partners and father the most pups. A powerful male Hooker's sea lion may mate with two dozen females in one season. A tough-fighting male Antarctic fur seal may have 50 to 100 partners, and a large bull southern elephant seal may mate with over 200 females. A female seal, or cow, wants the largest and strongest male to be her partner. In this way, her pup will inherit the good qualities of its father and have the best chance to survive.

The Weddell seal lives along the coast of Antarctica, farther south than any other seal.

Among land-breeding seals, males are larger—sometimes much larger—than their female partners. For example, a fur seal bull is often four to five times heavier than the female. The size difference is greatest in the elephant seals. A bull southern elephant seal may be ten times heavier than the female. Males need to be larger than the females because they fight so much. The bigger a seal is, the more males he can beat in a fight, and the more females he can win.

Ice-breeding seals, including harp seals, crabeaters, and Weddell seals, have an easier time mating. Most of the time, an ice-breeding male guards a single female until she is ready to mate. The males fight much less than land-breeding males, and as a result, they suffer fewer injuries. Among most of the ice-breeding seals, males and females are roughly the same size.

Seals
FUNFACT:

The most abundant seal in the world
is the crabeater seal. Scientists estimate that the total
population of crabeaters may exceed 20 million seals,
which is more than all the other species
of seals combined.

In most seals, the breeding season occurs around the same time the pups are being born. Usually a mother seal mates again within a few days to a few weeks after giving birth to a pup. Her next pup will be born approximately one year later, often on the same beach, and at the same time of the year. All male seals abandon their female partners soon after they mate with them. The fathers never care for their pups, and in fact, they probably never know them.

Seals
FUNFACT:

All seals molt their old fur and replace it with a fresh new coat every year. Most of them molt gradually, except for the elephant seals. When elephant seals molt, they stay on land and shed large patches of skin and fur that peel off their bodies like old paint from a building wall.

A male southern elephant seal may weigh ten times more than a female.
During mating, the male holds the female with his flipper and bites her on the neck.

On very crowded beaches, a newborn Hooker's sea lion may become separated from its mother, so it is very important for the two of them to quickly learn to recognize each other by their smell.

All seals give birth to a single pup. As soon as a pup is born, the mother spins around and nuzzles and sniffs her whining newborn. Mother fur seals are noisy, and they whimper and call to their pup. In a crowded seal colony, hundreds of pups may be born on the same day, and it is very important for a mother and a pup to recognize each other. They memorize the smell of each other's breath and the sound of each other's voices. Then, if they get separated, they can find each other easily with a sniff and a cry. Hungry pups will sometimes try to steal milk from a mother that is not their own. If they get sniffed and discovered, the angry mother may bite them and push them away.

Mother seals nurse and care for their pups in one of two ways: quickly or slowly. The earless seals, such as the hooded seal, the ringed seal, and the harbor seal are fast feeders. They nurse their pups with very rich, fatty milk. The milk is much thicker and has more fat than the thickest milkshake. The pups grow very quickly on such a fatty diet, and often double or triple their birth weight in less than two weeks. Then, when the pup looks like an overstuffed little sausage, the mother suddenly stops nursing and abandons it. Usually, the pup is only three or four weeks old. The shortest nursing period among all seals is seen in the hooded seal of the Arctic. The hooded seal pup nurses for just four days. In that short time, the silvery-blue pup balloons and doubles its birth weight, going from 44 pounds (20 kilograms) to 88 pounds (40 kilograms). It gains an amazing 11 pounds (5 kilograms) of fat every day. For humans to gain that much weight, they would have to gobble down 82 hamburgers and 23 large orders of french fries—every day for four days!

A nursing harp seal pup may suckle six or seven times a day.

Most earless seals are born on the surface of the sea ice in early spring. This cold, windy nursery is a dangerous place. Out in the open like this, the pups can easily be seen by predators such as arctic foxes and polar bears. To protect their pups, many mother seals give birth in areas of sea ice that frequently crack and break into pieces. Polar bears and foxes often stay away from this kind of ice because they don't want to fall into the cold water.

Because the ice may break at any moment, the seal pups face yet another danger. The newborn seals may be tossed into the icy water before they are big enough to swim and crawl out again. Because of this, an earless seal pup needs to grow very quickly and add a thick layer of blubber to keep its body warm if it should accidentally fall into the water.

Seals
FUNFACT:

The most playful of seals are young sea lions and fur seals. They chase each other, wrestle, and body surf. When there are no playmates, the young seals chew and play with pieces of driftwood, pebbles, or dried kelp—tossing the toys around and retrieving them.

This thin, young harp seal pup is waiting for its mother to return and nurse it. The adult seal in the water is ignoring the pup because it is probably not its mother.

A mother California sea lion will nurse her pup for one to three days, then leave it alone on the beach while she goes fishing for three to four days.

Fur seals and sea lions raise their families on land and do it differently than the ice-breeding seals. These seals raise their young slowly. Mother sea lions and fur seals produce milk that is less nourishing milk and contains less fat. As a result, their pups grow more slowly than the ice seals do, and the mothers must nurse them for many months. For example, a mother South American sea lion may nurse her pup for almost a year, and a mother Galapagos fur seal may nurse for two to three years.

Walrus mothers give birth on the ice in the same way as most of the earless seals, but the mothers raise their single pup like the fur seals and sea lions do. They stay with their pups for two years and nurse them throughout that time.

A bull walrus has few enemies, although scientists have seen them attacked and killed by large adult polar bears and killer whales.

Walruses feed by rooting along the ocean bottom, feeling for invertebrates (in-VER-tuh-brates), or small animals without backbones, with their sensitive whiskers. It takes a lot of practice for a young walrus to learn how to do this, so it needs to stay with its mother and nurse for several years before it can survive on its own.

The first few months of life are the most dangerous time for a pup. There is always the risk that it will become separated from its mother and starve to death. It may freeze to death in a frigid ice storm or drown when large waves wash over the beach. It can also be trampled to death by careless bulls fighting nearby. Once the pup reaches the age of one, it has a good chance to grow up to be an adult.

Adult life carries its own risks, and many predators have a taste for seal meat. In southern Africa, brown hyenas prey on sea lions that carelessly loaf along the beach at night. In South America, mountain lions hunt the rocky shorelines for unwary South American sea lions, and in British Columbia, coyotes stalk harbor seals along the coast. Some seals even eat their relatives. In the Arctic, bull walruses sometimes hunt and eat ringed seals, and in the Bering Sea of Alaska, hungry Steller sea lions kill young northern fur seals. In Antarctica, the leopard seal hunts fur seals, Weddell seals, Ross seals, and crabeaters. In fact, many adult crabeater seals have large scars on their sides or back from failed attacks by leopard seals.

Seals
FUNFACT:

Fur seals and sea lions are noisiest above the water, where they whimper, whine, bark, and roar. The earless seals, on the other hand, are usually quiet above the water but noisy underwater, where they warble, moan, buzz, chirp, and whistle.

This adult male Antarctic fur seal will not find a mate until it is at least seven years old. Until then, it stays on the edges of the colony and pretends to be tougher and bigger than it really is.

The biggest threat to all adult seals comes from in the ocean or beneath the ocean's surface. Wherever there are seal colonies, there are killer whales or great white sharks patrolling the waters offshore. No seal is too fast, too strong, or too large to be spared an attack by one of these fast-swimming hunters.

Both predators strike from below, rising out of the ocean blackness with speed and deadly force. Even shallow water doesn't keep them away. Great white sharks will attack elephant seals in waist-deep water, and killer whales in Argentina will throw themselves onto the beach to grab a sea lion resting by the water's edge.

Despite all the predators, the struggles to find food, and the battles of the breeding season, most seals survive to live for many years. Many seals live for 10 years or more, and some survive to the age of 25. The biggest threat to the survival of all seals comes from humans and the way they treat the oceans. When people pollute and overfish the oceans, it becomes more difficult for seals to survive. But it is never too late to make a change. Today, many people recognize that the health of the oceans is as important to the survival of humans as it is to the survival of seals. In the end, what is good for seals is also good for humans.

Internet Sites

You can find out more interesting information about seals and lots of other wildlife by visiting these web sites.

http://endangered.fws.gov/kids/index.html	U.S. Fish and Wildlife Service
www.animal.discovery.com	Discovery Channel Online
www.aqwa.com	The Aquarium of Western Australia
www.EnchantedLearning.com	Enchanted Learning
www.kidsplanet.org	Defenders of Wildlife
www.nationalgeographic.com/kids	National Geographic Society
www.nwf.org/kids	National Wildlife Federation
www.ocean.com/library/creaturefeature/	Ocean.com
www.pinnipeds.fsnet.co.uk	Seal Conservation Society
www.seaworld.org/Pinnipeds/introduction.html	Sea World Page
www.tnc.org	The Nature Conservancy
www.wcs.org	Wildlife Conservation Society
www.worldwildlife.org/ fun/kids.cfm	World Wildlife Fund
www.wwfcanada.org/satellite/wwfkids	Canadian World Wildlife Fund

Index

47

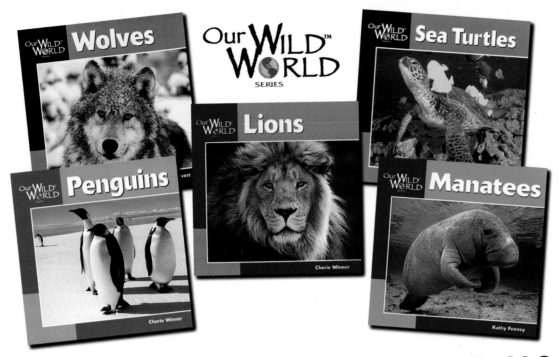

Paperback titles available in the Our Wild World Series:

BISON
ISBN 1-55971-775-0

BLACK BEARS
ISBN 1-55971-742-4

CARIBOU
ISBN 1-55971-812-9

COUGARS
ISBN 1-55971-788-2

DOLPHINS
ISBN 1-55971-776-9

EAGLES
ISBN 1-55971-777-7

LEOPARDS
ISBN 1-55971-796-3

LIONS
ISBN 1-55971-787-4

MANATEES
ISBN 1-55971-778-5

MOOSE
ISBN 1-55971-744-0

PENGUINS
ISBN 1-55971-810-2

POLAR BEARS
ISBN 1-55971-828-5

SEALS
ISBN 1-55971-826-9

SEA TURTLES
ISBN 1-55971-746-7

SHARKS
ISBN 1-55971-779-3

TIGERS
ISBN 1-55971-797-1

WHALES
ISBN 1-55971-780-7

WHITETAIL DEER
ISBN 1-55971-743-2

WOLVES
ISBN 1-55971-748-3

See your nearest bookseller, or order by phone 1-800-328-3895

NORTHWORD PRESS
Chanhassen, Minnesota